SandCastle 2

Homophones

The Knight
Waits at Night

Mary Elizabeth Salzmann

Publishing Company

Published by SandCastle™, an imprint of ABDO Publishing Company, 4940 Viking Drive, Edina, Minnesota 55435.

Cover and interior photo credits: Artville, Comstock, Corbis Images, Digital Stock, Digital Vision, Eyewire Images, PhotoDisc, Stockbyte

Library of Congress Cataloging-in-Publication Data

Salzmann, Mary Elizabeth, 1968-
　The knight waits at night / Mary Elizabeth Salzmann.
　　p. cm. -- (Homophones)
　Includes index.
　Summary: Photographs and simple text introduce homophones, words that sound alike but are spelled differently and have different meanings.
　ISBN 1-57765-651-2
　1. English language--Homonyms--Juvenile literature. [1. English language--Homonyms.] I. Title. II. Series.

PE1595 .S25 2002
428.1--dc21

2001053304

The SandCastle concept, content, and reading method have been reviewed and approved by a national advisory board including literacy specialists, librarians, elementary school teachers, early childhood education professionals, and parents.

Let Us Know

After reading the book, SandCastle would like you to tell us your stories about reading. What is your favorite page? Was there something hard that you needed help with? Share the ups and downs of learning to read. We want to hear from you! To get posted on the ABDO Publishing Company Web site, send us email at:

sandcastle@abdopub.com

About SandCastle™

Nonfiction books for the beginning reader

- Basic concepts of phonics are incorporated with integrated language methods of reading instruction. Most words are short, and phrases, letter sounds, and word sounds are repeated.

- Book levels are based on the ATOS™ for Books formula. Other considerations for readability include the number of words in each sentence, the number of characters in each word, and word lists based on curriculum frameworks.

- Full-color photography reinforces word meanings and concepts.

- "Words I Can Read" list at the end of each book teaches basic elements of grammar, helps the reader recognize the words in the text, and builds vocabulary.

- Reading levels are indicated by the number of flags on the castle.

SandCastle uses the following definitions for this series:

- Homographs: words that are spelled the same but sound different and have different meanings. *Easy memory tip: "-graph"= same look*

- Homonyms: words that are spelled and sound the same but have different meanings. *Easy memory tip: "-nym"= same name*

- Homophones: words that sound alike but are spelled differently and have different meanings. *Easy memory tip: "-phone"= sound alike*

Look for more SandCastle books in these three reading levels:

Level 1 (one flag)	**Level 2** (two flags)	**Level 3** (three flags)

Grades Pre-K to K 5 or fewer words per page	**Grades K to 1** 5 to 10 words per page	**Grades 1 to 2** 10 to 15 words per page

Note: Some pages in this book contain more than 10 words in order to more clearly convey the concept of the book.

knot

not

Homophones are words that sound alike but are spelled differently and have different meanings.

The baker kneads the bread dough.

Pam needs to practice
her flute.

He joined the navy.

He is a naval officer.

My navel shows when I wear my swimsuit.

Justine knows gymnastics.

She can do a back bend.

Peter got ice cream on
his nose.

I raise my hand when I know
the answer.

Charlie has caught no fish yet.

Andy reads the news and comics every day.

These animals are gnus.

Gnus live in Africa.

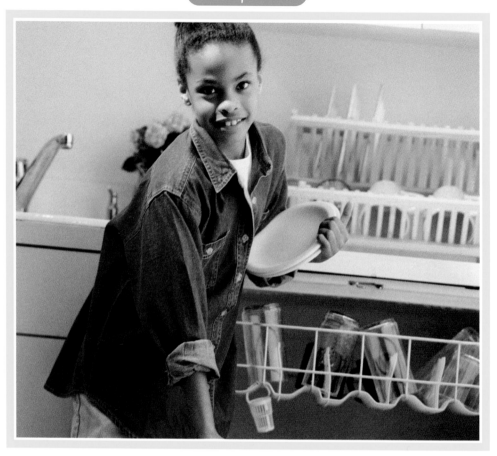

Tanya knew how to help.

My new puppy is soft.

Our favorite team is the New York Knicks.

Dad nicks **himself when he shaves.**

She is dressed like a nun.

How much milk is left?

(none)

Words I Can Read

Nouns

A noun is a person, place, or thing

answer (AN-sur) p. 12
back bend
 (BAK BEND) p. 10
baker (BAYK-ur) p. 6
bread (BRED) p. 6
day (DAY) p. 14
dough (DOH) p. 6
flute (FLOOT) p. 7

gymnastics
 (jim-NASS-tiks) p. 10
hand (HAND) p. 12
ice cream
 (EYESS KREEM) p. 11
knot (NOT) p. 4
milk (MILK) p. 21
navel (NAY-vuhl) p. 9
navy (NAY-vee) p. 8

news (NOOZ) p. 14
nose (NOHZ) p. 11
nun (NUHN) p. 20
officer (OF-uh-sur) p. 8
puppy (PUHP-ee) p. 17
swimsuit (SWIM-soot)
 p. 9
team (TEEM) p. 18

Plural Nouns

A plural noun is more than one person, place, or thing

animals
 (AN-uh-muhlz) p. 15
comics (KOM-ikss) p. 14
fish (FISH) p. 13

gnus (NOOZ) p. 15
homophones
 (HOME-uh-fonez) p. 5

meanings (MEE-ningz)
 p. 5
words (WURDZ) p. 5

Proper Nouns

A proper noun is the name of a person, place, or thing

Africa (AF-ruh-kuh) p. 15

Andy (AN-dee) p. 14

Charlie (CHAR-lee) p. 13

Dad (DAD) p. 19

Justine (JUHSS-teen) p. 10

New York Knicks (NOO YORK NIKSS) p. 18

Pam (PAM) p. 7

Peter (PEET-ur) p. 11

Tanya (TON-yuh) p. 16

Verbs

A verb is an action or being word

are (AR) pp. 5, 15

can (KAN) p. 10

caught (KAWT) p. 13

do (DOO) p. 10

dressed (DRESSD) p. 20

got (GOT) p. 11

has (HAZ) p. 13

have (HAV) p. 5

help (HELP) p. 16

is (IZ) pp. 8, 17, 18, 20, 21

joined (JOIND) p. 8

kneads (NEEDZ) p. 6

knew (NOO) p. 16

know (NOH) p. 12

knows (NOHZ) p. 10

left (LEFT) p. 21

live (LIV) p. 15

needs (NEEDZ) p. 7

nicks (NIKSS) p. 19

practice (PRAK-tiss) p. 7

raise (RAYZ) p. 12

reads (REEDZ) p. 14

shaves (SHAYVZ) p. 19

shows (SHOHZ) p. 9

sound (SOUND) p. 5

spelled (SPELD) p. 5

wear (WAIR) p. 9

Adjectives

An adjective describes something

alike (uh-LIKE) p. 5

different (DIF-ur-uhnt) p. 5

every (EV-ree) p. 14

favorite (FAY-vuh-rit) p. 18

her (HUR) p. 7

his (HIZ) p. 11

much (MUHCH) p. 21

my (MYE) pp. 9, 12, 17

naval (NAY-vuhl) p. 8

new (NOO) p. 17

no (NOH) p. 13

none (NUHN) p. 21

our (OUR) p. 18

soft (SAWFT) p. 17

these (THEEZ) p. 15

Match these homophones to the pictures

gnus
news

knight
night

naval
navel

none
nun